storecupboard checklist

D0453551

Don't run out of must-have basics – keep a list.

storecupboard checklist

favourite shops and suppliers

name

address

tel
fax
e-mail
www

name

address

tel
fax
e-mail
www

name

address

tel
fax
e-mail
www

name

address

tel
fax
e-mail
www

name

address

tel
fax
e-mail
www

name

address

tel
fax
e-mail
www

name

address

tel
fax
e-mail
www

name

address

tel
fax
e-mail
www

favourite shops and suppliers

name

address

tel

fax

e-mail

www

name

address

tel

fax

e-mail

www

name

address

tel

fax

e-mail

www

name

address

tel

fax

e-mail

www

name

address

tel

fax

e-mail

www

name

address

tel

fax

e-mail

www

name

address

tel

fax

e-mail

www

name

address

tel

fax

e-mail

www

useful websites and mail order

cookbooks and news

www.amazon.co.uk

Huge range of cookbooks, user-friendly food categories, discounts, interviews and reviews.

www.bol.com

Food and drink books, interviews, features, reviews, recommendations and discounts.

www.booksforcooks.com

Tel 020 7221 1992

info@booksforcooks.com

Huge range of worldwide food-related and cookery books, recipes, workshops. Mail order.

kitchenware and utensils

www.cucinadirect.co.uk

Tel 020 8246 4300

Beautiful china and glassware, top quality utensils, pans, knives, electrical appliances, tableware and gadgets. Also do mail order.

www.lakeland.co.uk

Tel 01539 488100

High quality kitchenware, tools, storage, electrical appliances and gourmet relishes. Also do mail order

www.thecookskitchen.com

Wide selection of quality kitchenware and equipment. Also do mail order.

www.johnlewis.com

Tel 020 7629 7711

Good value kitchenware, tools, gadgets, knives, pans, bar paraphernalia. Also do mail order.

groceries

www.waitrose.com

Home delivery, seasonal updates, specialist produce and groceries, special offers etc.

www.sainsburystoyou.com

Home delivery, recipes, reviews and special offers.

www.tesco.com

Home delivery, special offers, features, wine deals and produce information.

organic

www.simplyorganic.co.uk

Tel 0131 448 0440

All organic products, including fresh produce. Also do mail order.

www.freshfood.co.uk

Tel 020 8749 8778

Award winning shopping website, fresh produce, nationwide box scheme. Also do mail order.

gourmet and specialist

www.esperya.com

Tel (Italy) 00 39 010 726451

Fabulous regional Italian produce – charcuterie, cheese, wine, oil etc. Also do mail order.

www.teddingtoncheese.co.uk

Tel 020 8977 6868

Over 130 top quality British and Continental cheeses matured on the premises. Also do mail order.

www.shipton-mill.com

Long Newton, Tetbury, Glos GL8 8RP.

Tel 01666 505050

Huge range of bread flours, including organic, stoneground and specialist, favoured by craft bakers. Mail order only.

www.realcoffee.co.uk

Tel 01454 417147

Specialist coffee beans, blends, teas. Coffee information, recipes, advice. Also do mail order.

favourite websites

www
notes

www
notes

www
notes

www
notes

www
notes

www
notes

www
notes

www
notes

www
notes

www
notes

www
notes

www
notes

www
notes

www
notes

www
notes

www
notes

classic vinaigrette

Use this basic recipe just as it is, or adjust it
to suit your taste or mood.

5 tablespoons extra virgin olive oil
1 tablespoon white wine vinegar
1 teaspoon Dijon mustard (optional)
sea salt and freshly ground black pepper

makes about 125 ml

Put all the ingredients in a salad bowl and
beat with a fork or small whisk. Alternatively,
put in a screw-top bottle or small jar and
shake to form an emulsion.

variations

• Instead of 5 tablespoons extra virgin,
use 2 tablespoons mild virgin olive oil and
3 tablespoons nut oil, such as walnut
or hazelnut.

• Japanese rice vinegar gives a mild,
smooth taste. You can also substitute red
wine vinegar, sherry vinegar, cider vinegar,
or others. Freshly squeezed lime or lemon
juice are also traditional replacements
for the vinegar.

• A crushed garlic clove is often added to
vinaigrette. Delicious, but death to the breath.

• Some people like to include a little sugar in
the dressing, but this is only really necessary
if you have used too much vinegar.

• A warm vinaigrette poured over salad
leaves, meat, fish or vegetables is delicious.

• One of the nicest dressings of all is just a
sprinkle of best quality extra virgin olive oil.

Elsa Petersen-Schepelern

recipe

ingredients

method

source

recipe

ingredients

method

source

recipe

ingredients

method

source

recipe

ingredients

method

source

soups

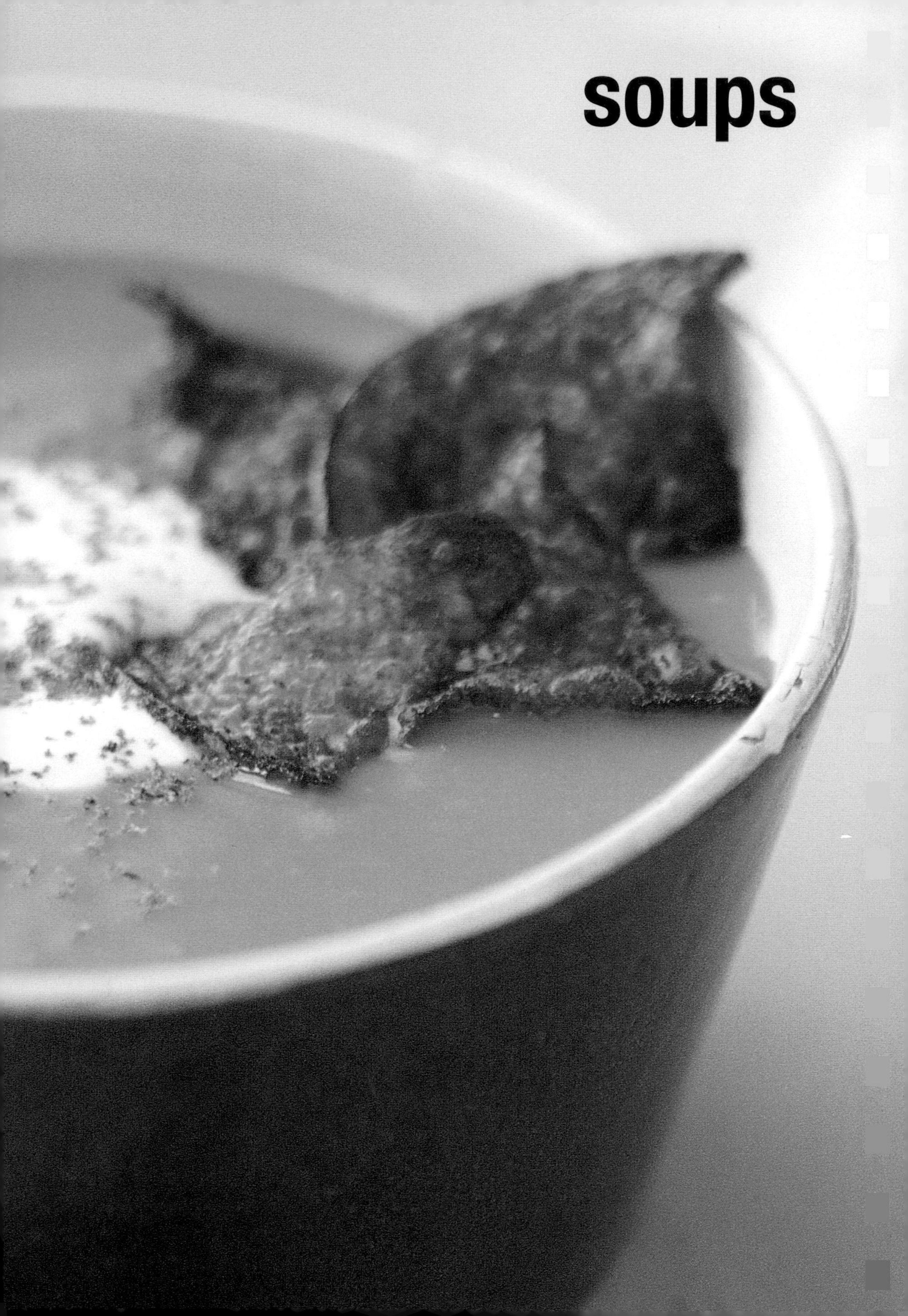

pumpkin soup with pumpkin crisps

The potatoes thicken the soup nicely and smooth the strong, very sweet taste of pumpkin. The milk is important – pumpkin loves milk – and it's also very fond of nutmeg.

1 kg pumpkin, deseeded and cut into large chunks

2 large potatoes, quartered

1 litre boiling chicken stock

50 g unsalted butter

2 tablespoons olive oil

2 large onions, finely sliced

250 ml milk

sea salt

pumpkin crisps

500 g pumpkin, deseeded but not peeled

sunflower oil

to serve

4 tablespoons sour cream

freshly grated nutmeg

serves 4

Put the pumpkin and potatoes in a large saucepan, add chicken stock or boiling water to cover, then simmer until tender. Drain, reserving the cooking liquid.

Heat the butter and oil in a frying pan, add the onions and fry until softened and lightly golden. Transfer to a blender or food processor, then add the pumpkin and potatoes, in batches if necessary. Blend, adding enough milk and cooking liquid to make a thick purée.

Transfer the purée to the saucepan and stir in enough stock to make a thick, creamy soup.

To make the pumpkin crisps, slice very thin sections off the pumpkin with a vegetable peeler, keeping an edge of skin on each if possible.

Fill a wok one-third full of sunflower oil or a deep-fryer to the manufacturer's recommended level. Heat to 190°C (375°F) or until a cube of bread browns in 30 seconds. Add the pumpkin slices in batches and fry until crisp and golden. Remove with a slotted spoon and drain on crumpled kitchen paper.

Add salt to the soup to taste, reheat without boiling, then ladle into heated soup bowls. Top with sour cream, nutmeg and a few pumpkin crisps.

Elsa Petersen-Schepelern

recipe

ingredients

method

source

recipe

ingredients

method

source

roasted chicken

A classic favourite, served with plenty of rich, garlic-and-wine-infused juices.

1.25–1.5 kg chicken

25 g unsalted butter

4 garlic cloves, well crushed

6 tablespoons robust red wine, such as Cabernet Sauvignon, Shiraz (Syrah), or Pinot Noir

sea salt and freshly ground black pepper

melted butter or olive oil, for brushing

serves 4

Put the butter and garlic in a small bowl and mix. Push some of the mixture under the breast skin and leg skin. Skewer the neck skin closed underneath. Sprinkle all over with salt and pepper.

Preheat the oven to 220° (425°F) Gas 7. Transfer the chicken to a roasting tin. Roast for 45 minutes, then reduce the heat to 190° (375°F) Gas 5 and roast for a further 30 minutes.

To test the chicken, pierce the thigh through the thickest part with a skewer. The juices should run clear and golden. If the juices still look at all pink, cook a little longer.

Transfer the chicken to a serving dish and put the dish in the oven. Turn off the heat and leave the door slightly open. Set the roasting tin on top of the stove over a high heat and stir in the wine, scraping up the sediment from the bottom of the tin. Boil down until syrupy, then serve with the chicken.

Clare Ferguson

roasting guide

Beef and lamb may be roasted to your taste, but pork, chicken and turkey must be roasted until cooked through: to test, insert a skewer into the thickest part (in poultry, this is the thigh). The juices should run clear or golden, never pink or bloody.

Beef

Pan-fry or roast at the highest temperature for 20 minutes, then roast at 190°C (375°F) Gas 5 for:

rare:	20 minutes per 500 g, plus 20 minutes
medium:	25 minutes per 500 g, plus 25 minutes
well done:	30 minutes per 500 g, plus 30 minutes.

Lamb

Pan-fry or roast at the highest temperature for 20 minutes, then roast at 190°C (375°F) Gas 5 for:

rare:	20 minutes per 500 g, plus 20 minutes
medium:	25 minutes per 500 g, plus 25 minutes
well done:	30 minutes per 500 g, plus 30 minutes.

Pork

Without crackling, roast at 170°C (325°F) Gas 3, 40 minutes per 500 g. With crackling, roast at the highest temperature for 30 minutes, then roast at 190°C (375°F) Gas 5 for 20 minutes per 500 g plus 20 minutes.

Chicken

Roast at 220°C (425°F) Gas 7 for 45 minutes, then reduce the heat and roast at 190°C (375°F) Gas 5 for 30 minutes.
Alternatively, roast at 200°C (400°F) Gas 6 for: 20 minutes per 500 g, plus 20 minutes.

Turkey

See *Celebrations* section.

recipe

ingredients

method

source

recipe

ingredients

method

source

recipe

ingredients

method

source

recipe

ingredients

method

source

beef

rare beef salad with parsley and wasabi mayonnaise

When you serve this, cut good, thick slices of beef about 1 cm wide. Increase the amount of fillet for the number of guests – since it's the same thickness, it will take the same amount of time in the oven, no matter how big it is.

1 beef fillet, about 50 cm long, well trimmed

250 g peppery leaves, such as watercress or rocket

sea salt and freshly ground black pepper

olive oil, for sealing

parsley oil

a bunch of parsley

250 ml extra virgin olive oil

wasabi mayonnaise

250 ml mayonnaise

2–3 tablespoons wasabi paste (about 1 tube)

serves 12

To make the parsley oil, put the parsley and olive oil in a blender and blend until smooth. Set aside for 30 minutes or overnight in the refrigerator.

Brush a heavy-based roasting tin with olive oil and heat on top of the stove until very hot. Add the beef and seal on all sides until nicely browned. Transfer to a preheated oven and roast at 200°C (400°F) Gas 6 for 20 minutes. Remove from the oven and set aside to fix the juices. Sprinkle with salt and pepper.

Let the meat cool to room temperature and reserve any cooking juices. If preparing in advance, wrap closely in foil and chill, but return it and the parsley oil to room temperature before serving.

Arrange the leaves down the middle of a rectangular or oval serving dish. Slice the beef into 1 cm thick slices with a very sharp carving knife (or an electric knife). Arrange in overlapping slices on top of the leaves and pour any cooking juices from the roasting tin or carving board over the top.

Drizzle the parsley oil, strained if necessary, over the beef. Mix the mayonnaise with the wasabi paste and serve separately.

Elsa Petersen-Schepelern

recipe

ingredients

method

source

recipe

ingredients

method

source

pork and lamb

char-grilled pork and aubergine

Based on Vietnamese and other South-east Asian flavours, this marinade is a flavour-enhancer for pork, but also happens to be wonderful with aubergine.

4 large or 8 small pork chops, boneless, about 750 g

2 medium aubergines

peanut oil, for brushing

marinade

125 ml fish sauce

2 tablespoons soy sauce

4 tablespoons sake or vodka

1 tablespoon chilli oil

to serve

mashed potatoes

mustard and cress

oven-roasted tomato halves (below)

serves 4

Put all the marinade ingredients in a wide, shallow dish, add the pork chops and turn to coat. Cover and chill for 1 hour or overnight, turning from time to time in the marinade.

When ready to cook, heat a large stove-top grill pan over medium heat until hot. If your pan is small, cook the aubergines first, keep them warm in the oven, then cook the pork chops.

Cut the aubergines lengthways into slices about 1 cm thick. Add the pork chops to the grill pan. Dip each slice of aubergine in the marinade and add to the grill pan in a single layer. Brush the chops and aubergine with marinade and leave, without disturbing, for about 5 minutes.

Brush the chops and aubergines with marinade again and turn them over to cook the other side. Brush the cooked side of the aubergines with peanut oil. Leave for another 5 minutes, or until the chops are cooked through.

To serve, put a dollop of mashed potatoes on each plate and put a pork chop on top. Arrange a share of the char-grilled aubergine on top, arranging each slice at 90 degrees to the previous one. Add 2–3 oven-roasted tomato halves, sprinkle with mustard and cress and serve.

If you have much marinade left over, bring it to the boil, simmer for 3 minutes, then drizzle over the dish.

To make oven-roasted tomato halves, cut 4 tomatoes in half crossways and put skin-side down into a roasting tray or shallow oven dish. Drizzle 2 tablespoons olive oil over the top and sprinkle with salt and black pepper. Roast in a preheated oven at 180°C (350°F) Gas 4 for 1 hour.

Elsa Petersen-Schepelern

marinades and rubs

Marinades and rubs can transform meat, chicken and fish cooked in a stove-top grill pan or on an outdoor barbecue. The difference between them is that a marinade is liquid and a rub is dry.

For all marinades, put the ingredients in a shallow dish, stir with a fork, then add the main ingredient and infuse for at least 30 minutes, or overnight, covered, in the refrigerator. Add oils, marinades and rubs to the food, not the pan.

For all rubs, mix all the ingredients together and rub onto meat, fish or poultry.

To prevent spices in dry rubs from burning, apply the rub on the meaty side only. Leave to penetrate for as long as possible, then cook the other side. When the food is almost cooked through, turn it over and cook the rubbed side, reducing the heat.

italian marinade

4 tablespoons olive oil

4 tablespoons red or white wine

4 tablespoons orange juice

a handful of fresh herbs, chopped

chinese marinade

3 cm fresh ginger, grated

4 spring onions, finely chopped

4 tablespoons soy sauce

2 tablespoons honey

2 whole star anise, crushed

ginger marinade

2 tablespoons peanut oil

2 cm fresh ginger, grated

1 tablespoon vodka

2 teaspoons 5-spice powder

1 teaspoon sea salt flakes

1 tablespoon chilli oil

vietnamese marinade

4 tablespoons fish sauce

4 tablespoons mirin

1 tablespoon sesame oil

5 cm fresh ginger, grated

moroccan yellow marinade

½ teaspoon ground ginger

2 teaspoons saffron powder

a pinch of cumin (optional)

2 tablespoons olive oil

saffron pepper

2 sachets saffron powder or
2 large pinches of saffron threads, toasted in a dry pan, then crushed

3 cm grated fresh ginger or
1 teaspoon ground ginger

1 tablespoon cracked
black pepper

paprika salt

1 tablespoon sweet or hot paprika

1 teaspoon sea salt

moroccan garlic rub

3 garlic cloves, crushed

5 cm fresh ginger, grated

½ teaspoon cumin seeds

2 tablespoons sweet paprika

1 teaspoon ground cinnamon

1 teaspoon cracked black pepper

2 teaspoons ground coriander

1 teaspoon salt

2 tablespoons brown sugar

chilli rub

1 teaspoon ground cumin

1 tablespoon ground coriander

2 teaspoons mustard seeds

4 tablespoons sweet paprika

4 tablespoons Kashmiri or ancho chilli powder

1 tablespoon sea salt

1 tablespoon freshly ground
black pepper

Put the cumin, coriander and mustard seeds in a dry frying pan and heat until aromatic and the seeds begin to pop. Remove from the heat and crush with a mortar and pestle. Mix with the remaining ingredients and use as a rub.

grill pan tips

Stove-top grill pans produce the delicious char-grilled flavours we usually associate with outdoor cooking. They cook food quickly and healthily – the ridges keep the food above and out of the fat.

• Heat the pan over a medium heat until it reaches the required temperature before you add the food.

• Oil the food, not the pan.

• Cook one side of the food thoroughly – so that the second side will need less time. This way, you can add spice rubs to the second side and the spices will be less likely to burn.

• For thicker foods, such as chicken, put a weight on top to ensure even contact with the pan. A saucepan half-filled with water works well.

• After you have added the food, leave it there. When it is ready to turn, it will move without sticking.

• Cool the pan before running under hot water to remove major particles. Then wash in the normal way – remembering that if the surface is non-stick or cast iron it shouldn't go in the dishwasher unless the manufacturer's instructions say it's O.K.

• Buy the biggest pan you can find – then you'll be able to cook a few grilled vegetables at the same time as the meat, fish or poultry – or even 2 whole fishes. The results are always delicious and crispy.

Elsa Petersen-Schepelern

recipe

ingredients

method

source

recipe

ingredients

method

source

fish

barbecued salmon steaks
with basil and parmesan butter

Watch the steaks carefully while cooking – they can easily overcook. Brushing the bars of the grill with a little oil will prevent the salmon from sticking. We should use flavoured butters more: they are delicious.

6 fresh salmon steaks, cut about 2 cm thick, 1.5 kg total weight

basil parmesan butter

175 g unsalted butter

25 g freshly grated Parmesan cheese

1 teaspoon balsamic or sherry vinegar

25 g fresh basil leaves, sliced

freshly ground black pepper

marinade

1 large garlic clove, crushed

150 ml light olive oil

2 tablespoons balsamic or sherry vinegar

1–2 sprigs of thyme, crushed

serves 6

To make the basil and Parmesan butter, beat the butter until soft. Gradually beat in the grated Parmesan, vinegar, basil leaves and ground black pepper to taste. Scoop onto to a piece of wet greaseproof paper and roll into a cylinder. Wrap in clingfilm and refrigerate (or freeze) for at least 1 hour, or until firm.

Put the marinade ingredients in a wide, shallow dish, mix well, then add the salmon steaks and turn to coat well. Cover and let marinate for 20–30 minutes. Lift the steaks from the marinade and pat dry with kitchen paper.

Heat a barbecue until the coals are MEDIUM hot and white (no longer red). Lightly oil the grill bars, add the salmon and barbecue for about 3 minutes on each side until crisp and brown on the outside and just opaque all the way through – overcooked salmon is dry, so be careful to cook it properly. Serve the salmon steaks covered with slices of the chilled butter melting on top.

Note: If using other herbs, such as parsley, tarragon or marjoram, always use fresh: dried herbs have less flavour and tend to have a musty taste.

Maxine Clark

recipe

ingredients

method

source

recipe

ingredients

method

source

recipe

ingredients

method

source

recipe

ingredients

method

source

pasta tips

• When cooking pasta, bring a large saucepan of water to the boil, add a pinch of salt, then add the pasta to the boiling water. Boil with the lid off until done. Don't overcook, or the pasta will lose its springy, chewy quality. It should be slightly firm to the bite – *al dente* in Italian.

• To cook fresh pasta, add it to a saucepan of boiling water and cook just until the pasta rises to the surface (a matter of moments). If cooking filled fresh pasta, continue cooking for a little longer, to heat the filling through. The time depends on the kind of filling, but is about 30 seconds to 1 minute more. Drain and serve.

• Dried pasta is made with or without egg. Egg-based pasta has a silkier texture and richer taste than regular and generally goes well with butter- or cream-based sauces. Plain is best with oil-based sauces.

• Match the shape of pasta to the sauce. Delicate, liquid sauces need long strands or ribbons, whereas chunky or meaty sauces go well with short tubes or shells – the sauce catches in the hollows.

• Never add olive oil to the cooking water. It is a waste of good oil.

• Be careful not to overdrain pasta, and never rinse it. In order for the sauce to cling, the pasta needs the slippery coating from its starchy cooking water.

classic tomato sauce

A quick, everyday recipe for pasta – it can be stored in the refrigerator until needed.

2 tablespoons olive oil

1 onion, chopped

3 garlic cloves, chopped

500 g canned chopped tomatoes

1 teaspoon balsamic vinegar

1 teaspoon sugar

salt and freshly ground black pepper

serves 4

Heat the oil in a frying pan. Add the onion and fry gently until translucent. Add the garlic and fry until fragrant. Add the tomatoes, vinegar and sugar and simmer gently for 15–20 minutes. Season to taste.

Optional extras: chopped chilli (added with the onion), a splash of red wine, Madeira, port or vermouth (added with the tomatoes) or torn basil leaves (added in the last minute of cooking).

pesto

Italy's famous basil-based sauce is traditionally made with a mortar and pestle, but it is now more often made in a food processor.

a large bunch of basil

100 g pine nuts, lightly toasted in a dry frying pan

2 garlic cloves

50 g freshly grated Parmesan cheese

6 tablespoons olive oil

sea salt and freshly ground black pepper

serves 4

Put the basil, pine nuts, garlic and Parmesan in a food processor and blend. Drizzle in the olive oil little by little. Season to taste.

Note: To make pesto with a mortar and pestle, pound the garlic and pine nuts with a pinch of sea salt. Pound in the basil, a quarter at a time. Pound in the cheese until mixed. Beat in the olive oil to make a thick, creamy paste.

Celia Brooks Brown

recipe

ingredients

method

source

recipe

ingredients

method

source

recipe

ingredients

method

source

recipe

ingredients

method

source

rice

rice types and cooking methods

White Long Grain A useful, all-purpose and everyday rice. Follow packet instructions to cook, 12–15 minutes.

Brown Long Grain Has a chewy texture and nutty flavour, and makes a substantial savoury dish or accompaniment. Cooking time is longer than white, about 45–50 minutes – follow packet instructions.

Italian Risotto Rice (carnaroli, arborio) Plump and tender and makes a sumptuous, creamy risotto with separate grains. Cooks in 18–20 minutes, but with risotto method of adding hot liquid in stages, takes a total of 25–30 minutes.

Pudding Rice Sticky and soft, good for sweet dishes, especially moulded puddings, as the grains cling together. Takes about 15 minutes, but longer in the oven.

White Basmati Rice Long, slim grain with clean scent and wonderful aroma, grains stay separate. Considered by many to be the world's finest rice, perfect for savoury dishes. Cooks in 10–12 minutes – follow packet instructions.

Brown Basmati Rice Dense, chewy texture and nutty flavour. Store in a cool, dark place or refrigerate as natural oils can become rancid. Cooks in 45–60 minutes, according to packet instructions.

Thai Fragrant Rice Favourite everyday rice of South-east Asian cooks. Slight stickiness, and good with curries and stir-fries. Cooks in 12–15 minutes, or according to packet instructions. Some people rinse the cooked rice under boiling water to separate clumps.

Japanese Sushi Rice Sticky, absorbent and ideal for sushi, where the grains must stick together. Cooks in 15–20 minutes plus standing time, or follow packet instructions.

Wild Rice Not a true rice, but an aquatic grass. Nutty, earthy taste works well with game, poultry and seafood. When fully cooked it may 'flower' or 'butterfly' – one or both ends spring apart to reveal the white interior. Swells to 2½–4 times original volume when cooked. Cooks in 55–60 minutes, or according to packet instructions.

Clare Ferguson

risotto with four cheeses

The stock in risotto should always be added hot and in stages, never all at once – the rice needs time to absorb each ladle of stock before the next one is added. Another golden rule of risotto is to keep stirring all the time – don't wander off!

900 ml vegetable or chicken stock

50 g unsalted butter

1 tablespoon olive oil

8 shallots, finely chopped

1 garlic clove, crushed

275 g risotto rice, such as vialone nano, carnaroli or arborio

1 glass white wine, about 125 ml

100 g Parmesan cheese, freshly grated, plus extra to serve

50 g Gorgonzola cheese, cut into cubes

50 g Fontina cheese, cut into cubes

50 g Taleggio cheese, rind removed and cheese cut into cubes

a handful of flat leaf parsley, coarsely chopped

sea salt and freshly ground black pepper

serves 4

Put the stock in a saucepan. Heat until almost boiling, then reduce the heat until barely simmering to keep it hot.

Heat the butter and oil in a sauté pan or heavy-based casserole over a medium heat. Add the shallots and cook for 1–2 minutes, until softened but not browned. Add the garlic and mix well.

Add the rice and stir, using a wooden spoon, until the grains are well coated and glistening, about 1 minute. Pour in the wine and stir until it has been completely absorbed.

Add 1 ladle of hot stock and simmer, stirring until it has been absorbed. Continue to add the stock at intervals and cook as before, until the liquid has been absorbed and the rice is tender but still firm (*al dente*), about 18–20 minutes. Reserve the last ladle of stock.

Add the reserved stock, cheeses, parsley, salt and pepper. Mix well. Remove from the heat, cover and let rest for 2 minutes.

Spoon into warmed bowls, sprinkle with Parmesan and serve.

Ursula Ferrigno

recipe

ingredients

method

source

recipe

ingredients

method

source

noodles

noodle types and cooking times

wheat flour noodles

Chinese Wheat Noodles
fresh: rinse in warm water, then boil
for 3–4 minutes
dried: boil for 4–5 minutes.

egg and wheat flour noodles

Chinese Thick Wheat Noodles
fresh: rinse in warm water, then boil
for 3–4 minutes
dried: boil for 7–9 minutes.

Chinese Thin Wheat Noodles
fresh: rinse in warm water, then boil
for 1½–2 minutes
dried: boil for 4½–5 minutes.

rice flour noodles

Rice Ribbon Noodles
Used in China and South-east Asia. Also
known as *ho fun* (Chinese) or *banh pho*
(Vietnamese).
fresh: soak in hot water to separate, then
cook for 1 minute
dried: boil for 2–3 minutes.

Thai Broad Rice Stick Noodles
Broad, flat noodles. Also known as *sen yai*.
fresh: soak in hot water to separate,
then boil for 1 minute
dried: soften in hot water for 15 minutes,
then boil for 2–3 minutes.

Chinese Rice Stick or Vermicelli Noodles
always dried: soften in hot water for
15 minutes, then boil for 1 minute.
Alternatively, deep-fry for 30 seconds.

Thai Thin Rice Vermicelli Noodles
For soups, salads, spring rolls. Known as *bun*.
always dried: Stir-fry or boil for 1–2 minutes,
or deep-fry briefly until crisp but still pale.

Thai Fine Rice Stick Vermicelli Noodles
Very fine and hair-like, also known as *banh hoi*.
always dried: soften in hot water for
5 minutes, then steam for 5 minutes.

egg and rice flour noodles

Thai Egg and Rice Flour Noodles
Sold in nests that are shaken loose before
cooking. Also known as *ba mee*.
always fresh: rinse in warm water, then boil
for 3–4 minutes.

beanthread noodles

Cellophane, Glass or Beanthread Noodles
Made from mung bean flour. Available in
various widths from wide and ribbon-like to
fine wire-like threads.
always dried: Soften in warm water for
15 minutes, then boil or stir-fry for 1 minute.

japanese noodles

Soba Noodles (buckwheat flour)
fresh: rinse in warm water, then boil
for 1–1½ minutes
dried: boil for 5–6 minutes.

Udon Noodles (wheat flour)
fresh: rinse in warm water, then boil
for 1–2 minutes
dried: boil for 10–12 minutes.

Ramen Noodles (egg and wheat flour)
fresh: rinse in warm water, then boil
for 1–2 minutes
dried: boil for 4½–5 minutes.

Somen Noodles (wheat flour)
fresh: rinse in warm water, then boil
for 1–2 minutes.
dried: boil for 2½–3 minutes.

Joy Davies

chilled soba noodle salad

Soba noodles are made from buckwheat and are firmer than other noodles. Other Japanese noodles are also delicious served cold – you could substitute white somen noodles, or the larger, ribbon-like udons.

400 g soba noodles

12 dried shiitake mushrooms

2 tablespoons soy sauce

2 tablespoons mirin

12 uncooked prawns

12 spring onions, finely sliced

4 tablespoons wasabi paste

dipping sauce

250 ml dashi stock

125 ml Chinese rice wine
or ginger wine

serves 4

Simmer the sauce ingredients in a saucepan for 5 minutes, then chill. Cook the noodles according to the packet instructions, then drain, rinse in cold water and cool quickly over ice. Chill.

Put the shiitakes in a saucepan, cover with 250 ml boiling water and soak until soft. Remove and discard the mushroom stems. Add the soy sauce and mirin to the pan, bring to the boil and simmer for a few minutes until the liquid is slightly reduced. Cool and chill.

Poach the prawns in simmering salted water for about 1 minute until firm, then peel them, leaving the tail fins intact. Devein and split each prawn down the back to the fin, giving a butterfly shape. Chill.

Put the noodles in a bowl. Add ice cubes and top with the prawns, spring onions and mushrooms. Pour over the mushroom cooking liquid. Serve with separate dishes of wasabi paste and dipping sauce.

Elsa Petersen-Schepelern

recipe

ingredients

method

source

recipe

ingredients

method

source

recipe

ingredients

method

source

recipe

ingredients

method

source

classic egg recipes

boiled eggs

Ideally, bring the eggs to room temperature before cooking. Put the eggs into a saucepan and add cold water to cover. Put the pan over high heat and bring to the boil. Reduce to a low simmer for 3 minutes for very soft eggs with the white not quite set, 4 minutes for the white to be set but the yolk still runny and 5 minutes for both yolk and white to be set. Drain and serve.

poached eggs

Crack the eggs into individual cups. Bring a large saucepan of water to the boil. Add 1 tablespoon clear vinegar, and reduce to a gentle simmer. Swirl the water in one direction with a fork to create a whirlpool effect. Gently slip each egg into the water, return to a gentle simmer, then cover, remove from the heat and let stand for 6–7 minutes, depending on how well-done you like the yolks. Remove the eggs with a slotted spoon, put the spoon with the egg onto a piece of kitchen paper to drain for 20 seconds, then serve.

fried eggs

For 2 eggs, heat 2 tablespoons olive oil in a small frying pan. When very hot, crack the eggs, one at a time, into the pan, reduce the heat and cook, using a spoon to baste the eggs with the oil, tipping the pan slightly to catch it. When the white is cooked through, slide a slotted egg lifter under each egg, remove and serve.

omelette

Break the eggs, 2 or 3 per omelette, into a bowl and add black pepper to taste. Beat briefly with a fork. Melt 1 tablespoon butter in a frying pan. When it stops frothing, swirl in the egg. Lightly fork through the mixture a couple of times to allow the liquid egg to run into the spaces. As soon as it is set on the bottom, but is still a little runny in the middle (it will carry on cooking off the heat), sprinkle with salt to taste. Transfer to a warmed plate, folding the omelette in half as you go. Serve immediately.

cheese tips

Cheese is usually made from cows', sheeps' or goats' milk. Within these types there is a huge range of sizes, textures and tastes – from a soft, mild, goats' cheese, which is made to be consumed on the same day, to hard, strong Parmesan, which can be matured for 4 years.

buying

• Buy ripe cheese – it will not ripen properly at home. Where possible, buy from a specialist cheese merchant, so you can taste the cheeses before you buy.

• Buy little and often. Many cheeses go off quickly and are best eaten soon after buying.

storing

• Wrap cheese in waxed paper, never clingfilm. It needs to breathe, and waxed paper allows for this. For the same reason, wrap it loosely.

• Ideally, store cheese in a cool, ventilated place. A garage or cellar provide better conditions than a warm kitchen, but if you don't have such places, the warmest part of the refrigerator is the best option.

• If storing cheese in the refrigerator, remove it to room temperature at least 30 minutes before eating – the flavours and textures are affected if the cheese is too cold.

• The harder the cheese, the longer it will keep.

• Hard cheeses, such as Parmesan, Stilton and Cheddar, can be frozen, in wrapped wedges. Do not freeze soft cheeses, as the flavour is damaged while they are defrosting.

cheese

recipe

ingredients

method

source

recipe

ingredients

method

source

recipe

ingredients

method

source

recipe

ingredients

method

source

spanish roasted vegetables

A classic Spanish dish full of country richness and sweet summer bounty, although it is still possible to make it well into late autumn. It can be served as a hot, warm or cool salad.

2 red peppers

2 yellow peppers

½ butternut squash or
500 g pumpkin, unpeeled

2 red onions, unpeeled

2 Spanish onions, unpeeled

4 medium, vine-ripened tomatoes

125 ml extra virgin olive oil,
preferably Spanish

sea salt and freshly ground
black pepper

serves 4–6

Cut the peppers in half lengthways, slicing through the stems. Leave these intact but discard the pith and seeds.

Slice the butternut or pumpkin, into 2.5 cm discs or chunks.

Cut the onions crossways into halves, leaving the roots and tops intact. Leave the skins on too – they give extra colour and flavour and protect the shape.

Put all the vegetables, cut sides up, in a large, lightly oiled roasting tin. Drizzle half the oil over the vegetables and sprinkle with sea salt and pepper.

Roast towards the top of a preheated oven at 240°C (475°F) Gas 9 for 30 minutes, until the vegetables are frizzled, fragrant, wrinkled and soft.

Drizzle the remaining oil over the top and serve hot, warm or cool. Eat the salad with your fingers, discarding the skins, roots and stems along the way.

Note: Use bread to scoop up the sweet, oily, sticky juices.

Clare Ferguson

classic potato recipes

perfect roasted potatoes

Peel and cut the potatoes into even sizes and put into a large saucepan. Cover with cold water and bring to the boil. Reduce the heat and simmer for 8 minutes. Drain well and return the potatoes to the pan. Holding the lid on, shake the pan vigorously to roughen the outsides of the potatoes.

Meanwhile, pour 175 ml olive oil (for 1 kg potatoes) into a roasting tin. Put into a preheated oven at 220°C (425°F) Gas 7 for 5 minutes. Using a long-handled spoon, add the drained potatoes carefully to the hot oil and move them around to coat. Roast in the oven for 50–60 minutes until crisp and golden, turning from time to time to stop the potatoes sticking.

perfect mashed potatoes

Peel and cut the potatoes into large, evenly-sized chunks. Put them in a saucepan, add water to cover, and a good pinch of salt, then bring to the boil. Reduce the heat and simmer for 20 minutes until tender. Drain and return the potatoes to the pan over a very low heat. Steam until dry, then remove from the heat. Mash thoroughly. Add plenty of butter and warm milk and beat with a wooden spoon until smooth. Add salt and pepper to taste, plus any other flavourings, such as freshly grated nutmeg, mustard or chopped herbs. Mix well and serve.

perfect chips

Peel and cut the potatoes into finger-sized pieces. Rinse in cold water to remove excess starch and dry well with kitchen paper. Transfer to a deep-fryer basket.

Half fill a deep-fryer or large saucepan with sunflower oil and heat to approximately 180°C (360°F), or until a cube of bread browns in 60 seconds. Plunge the vegetables into the oil and cook for 5 minutes, until tender but still pale. Remove and drain on kitchen paper. Increase the heat to approximately 195°C (385°F), or until a cube of bread browns in 20 seconds. Cook the chips again for 2–3 minutes until golden. Remove, tip onto a plate with a layer of kitchen paper on top, sprinkle with salt and serve.

vegetable tips

Freshly picked vegetables that taste good are bursting with life and colour. The roots should be springy, the leaves a vibrant green and there should be no soft or wrinkled patches. Don't be put off by irregular shapes and sizes – uniformity is not an indication of flavour and quality.

buying

• Choose courgettes, peppers and aubergines which are firm, glossy and wrinkle-free. They should be heavy for their size.

• Beans and carrots should be firm and will snap rather than bend when you break them in half.

• Make sure that onions and garlic feel firm and have no shoots.

storing

• Never keep tomatoes in the refrigerator – it spoils their texture and flavour. Put them next to the kitchen window, where they will ripen.

• Store carrots, courgettes, aubergines, peppers, peas, beans, asparagus, salad leaves and cucumbers in the salad drawer of the refrigerator.

• Keep potatoes in a cool, dark place, but not the refrigerator. If left too long in the light, they start to turn green and produce shoots. Green potatoes should not be eaten.

• Never put avocados in the refrigerator.

• Eat broad beans, peas and corn as soon as possible after buying, ideally the same day – their flavour and texture deteriorate quickly after being picked.

recipe

ingredients

method

source

recipe

ingredients

method

source

recipe

ingredients

method

source

recipe

ingredients

method

source

chocolate chunk nut cookies

Simple to make, crisp on the outside, soft and gooey in the middle, with an absolutely divine taste – what more could you ask for? Vary the nuts to suit yourself: walnuts or hazelnuts work well, but you can also use pecans, macadamias and pine nuts. Keep the chocolate and nuts chunky for maximum impact.

Put all the ingredients, except the chocolate and nuts, in a food processor and blend until mixed. Stir in the chocolate and nuts. Alternatively, sift the flour, baking powder and salt into a bowl. Put the butter, sugar and vanilla in another bowl and beat with a wooden spoon or electric mixer, until light and fluffy. Gradually beat in the egg. Fold in the flour mixture, then mix in the chocolate and nuts.

Scrape the cookie dough onto a large square of clingfilm and roll into a 30 cm long sausage shape. Twist the ends to seal and chill for at least 30 minutes or until firm.

When ready to bake, unwrap the dough and cut into 2 cm thick slices. Put 3 cm apart on the prepared baking sheet (in batches, if necessary) and bake in a preheated oven at 190°C (375°F) Gas 5 for 15–20 minutes, until just golden. Transfer to a wire rack to cool.

Celia Brooks Brown

125 g plain flour

½ teaspoon baking powder

½ teaspoon salt

125 g unsalted butter, softened

100 g soft brown sugar

1 teaspoon vanilla extract

1 egg

200 g plain chocolate, (70 per cent cocoa solids) coarsely chopped

50 g nuts, such as pecans or hazelnuts, coarsely chopped

a large baking sheet, lined with baking parchment

makes 12–14

gooey brownies

Try these warm for pudding – straight from the oven, with a dollop of extra thick cream and a handful of raspberries. Alternatively, let them cool and eat them any time of day. Be careful not to overcook – brownies should be slightly gooey in the middle.

115 g unsalted butter, softened

300 g caster sugar

1 teaspoon vanilla extract

5 large eggs, beaten

70 g plain flour

70 g cocoa powder

230 g plain chocolate, melted and cooled

1 cake tin, about 22.5 x 27.5 cm, greased and base lined

makes 30

Beat the butter with the sugar until soft and fluffy then beat in the vanilla extract. Gradually beat in the eggs, a little at a time. Sift the flour with cocoa into the bowl and stir in. Mix in the melted chocolate. Spoon into the prepared tin and spread evenly.

Bake in a preheated oven at 170°C (325°F) Gas 3 for about 20 minutes until almost firm to the touch. Leave to cool then cut into tiny squares and remove from the tin. Store in an airtight container and eat within 3 days.

Linda Collister

chocolate tips

choosing

• For best taste and final results choose dark, plain chocolate labelled 'continental style', with cocoa solids around 70 per cent, and pure vanilla extract.

storing

• Store chocolate away from other foods in a cool, dry spot. Avoid storing in the refrigerator or below 13°C as beads of moisture will form as it returns to room temperature.

chopping and grating

• In warm weather, chill the chocolate until firm before you start, then use the large-hole side of the grater for grating. Use a clean, dry board and a large knife for chopping.

• Chocolate can also be chopped in a processor using the pulse button – take care not to overwork the chocolate or it can turn warm and sticky.

• When chopping chocolate for melting it's important that the chocolate is cut into evenly sized pieces, so it all melts at the same rate.

melting

• Melt chocolate slowly and gradually in the top of a double boiler, or in a heatproof bowl set over a saucepan of simmering water. Take care: it easily becomes overheated and scorched and turns into a solid lump.

• Alternatively, melt in a microwave. Start at 30 seconds and test often. The pieces will not lose their shape.

recipe

ingredients

method

source

recipe

ingredients

method

source

pastry tips

• Make sure everything is as cold as possible before you start – the ingredients as well as your hands.

• Sift the flour into the food processor or bowl – good pastry is made with aerated flour.

• Handle pastry as little as possible. If making by hand, rub the fat into the flour with your fingertips, but use a round-bladed knife when you add water.

• Work quickly, making sure you don't overwork or overstretch the pastry, or the result will be a tough and heavy dough.

• Resting the pastry in the refrigerator before rolling is essential. The dough heats up as you work on it – chilling allows it to cool and rest so that it won't shrink too much while it cooks.

• When rolling out pastry, dust both the work surface and the rolling pin with flour, re-dusting as needed.

• Flute the rim of the uncooked pastry case gently with your fingers to match the fluting on the sides of the tart tin.

• For crisp pasty, the tart case should be baked blind before filling. To bake blind, line the tin with pastry, then with paper. Add dried beans or uncooked rice and bake in a preheated oven at 200°C (400°F) Gas 6 for 15 minutes until pale gold. Lower the temperature to 180°C (350°F) Gas 4. Remove the paper and beans and return the pastry to the oven for 5 minutes to dry out the base.

• Unrolled pastry keeps wrapped in the refrigerator for up to 3 days, and for up to 3 months in the freezer.

basic sweet tart

Once you have the basic sweet pastry case, you can fill it with anything you fancy. Try the lemon filling below, or simply fill it with whipped cream and seasonal fruits, cut into pieces.

150 g plain flour

a pinch of salt

25 g golden caster sugar

85 g unsalted butter, chilled and diced

1 large egg yolk

1–2 tablespoons iced water

a 23 cm loose-based flan or tart tin

non-stick baking parchment

ceramic baking beans, dried beans or uncooked rice

serves 6

Put the flour, salt, sugar and butter into a food processor and process until it looks like fine crumbs. With the machine running, add the egg yolk and water through the tube and process just until the dough comes together. Wrap and chill for about 30 minutes.

Roll out the dough on a lightly floured surface to a circle about 28 cm across. Use to line the flan tin, prick the bottom of the pastry case with a fork, then chill for 15 minutes.

Cut a round of non-stick baking parchment the same size as the pastry lining the tin and gently press into the pastry case to cover the base and sides. Fill the lined case with ceramic baking beans, dried beans or uncooked rice and bake in a preheated oven at 200°C (400°F) Gas 6 for 15 minutes until lightly golden.

Remove the paper and beans and lower the temperature to 180°C (350°F) Gas 4. Bake for 5–7 minutes until crisp and lightly golden. If adding the lemon filling, below, reduce the oven temperature to 160°C (325°F) Gas 3, and put a baking sheet in the oven to preheat.

lemon filling

3 large eggs plus 1 yolk

150 ml double cream

100 g golden caster sugar

grated zest of 2 large, unwaxed lemons

freshly squeezed juice of 3 large lemons

a baking sheet

serves 6

Put all the ingredients into a large jug and beat, by hand, until just combined. Set the prepared, pre-baked pastry case, in the flan tin, on a preheated baking sheet and pour in three-quarters of the filling. Put into the preheated oven at 160°C (325°F) Gas 3, then carefully pour in the remaining filling (this way you avoid spilling the filling as you put the tart into the oven).

Bake for 25–30 minutes or until the filling is firm when the tart is gently shaken. Let cool before unmoulding. Serve at room temperature or chilled.

Linda Collister

apple and berry deep dish pie

Apples don't need any cooking before going into a pie, or they will reduce to a slush. Just make sure they are crisp and tart.

180 g plain flour

a good pinch of salt

1 teaspoon golden caster sugar

90 g unsalted butter, chilled and diced

about 4 tablespoons iced water, to bind

apple and berry filling

about 900 g Bramleys or crisp tart eating apples, peeled, cored and thickly sliced or diced

250 g raspberries, mulberries, loganberries or tayberries

2 tablespoons golden caster sugar, or to taste

a deep, oval pie dish, about 22 cm long

serves 6

Put the flour, salt, sugar and butter into a food processor and process until the mixture looks like fine crumbs. With the machine running, gradually add the water through the feed tube to make a soft but not sticky dough. Wrap and chill.

Put the apples and berries into a bowl, add a little sugar to taste and mix gently. If the apples are not juicy, add a tablespoon of water or lemon juice. Spoon the fruit into the pie dish, heaping it up in the middle to support the pastry.

Turn the dough onto a lightly floured work surface and roll it into an oval about 7.5 cm larger than your pie dish all the way around. Cut off a strip of dough about 1 cm wide, and long enough to go around the rim of the dish. Dampen the rim and paste on the strip of dough, joining the ends neatly. Dampen this pastry rim. Carefully cover the pie with the rest of the pastry, pressing it onto the rim to seal.

With a sharp knife, trim the excess dough and use to decorate the top. Push up the sides of the crust with a small knife, then crimp or flute the pastry rim. Make a steam hole in the centre, then bake the pie in a preheated oven at 200°C (400°F) Gas 6 for about 30 minutes until the pastry is crisp and golden. Sprinkle with sugar and serve warm or at room temperature.

Linda Collister

recipe

ingredients

method

source

recipe

ingredients

method

source

recipe

ingredients

method

source

recipe

ingredients

method

source

puddings

blackberry and raspberry sorbet

The difference between ice cream and sorbet is that ice cream is made using cream or milk and egg yolks, whereas the basic ingredients of a sorbet are sugar, fruit and water. Adjust the sweetness to suit your taste, adding more sugar before churning if necessary. You can make sorbets with your choice of fruit juices or purées.

500 g blackberries

250 g raspberries

grated zest and juice of 1 lemon

400 g sugar, or to taste

water (see method)

2 tablespoons Framboise (optional)

1–2 egg whites, beaten (optional)

makes about 1 litre

Put the blackberries, raspberries, lemon zest and juice and sugar into a saucepan. Bring slowly to the boil and simmer for about 2 minutes, then remove from the heat.

Strain into a measuring jug, pressing as much fruit as possible through the sieve. If necessary, add water to achieve 1 litre of pulp. Cool, and stir in the Framboise, if using. Taste and add extra sugar if preferred, then chill. Fold the beaten egg whites, if using, into the berry mixture.

Transfer to an ice cream making machine and churn. Serve immediately, or freeze.

Note: If you don't have an ice cream maker, you can still make sorbets and ice cream. Just pour the mixture into flat freezer trays, allow it to part-freeze, then beat to break up the ice crystals and return to the freezer. Repeat several times – the more often you do it, the smoother the end result.

Elsa Petersen-Schepelern

recipe

ingredients

method

source

recipe

ingredients

method

source

recipe

ingredients

method

source

recipe

ingredients

method

source

preserving tips

sterilization of preserving jars

• It is essential for safety reasons that jars are sterilized before they are filled with jam or chutney.

• Wash the jars in hot, soapy water and rinse in boiling water. Put into a large saucepan and then cover with hot water. With the lid on, bring the water to the boil and continue boiling for 15 minutes. Turn off the heat, then leave the jars in the hot water until just before they are to be filled. Invert the jars onto a clean cloth to dry. Sterilize the lids for 5 minutes, by boiling, or according to the manufacturer's instructions. The jars should be filled and sealed while they are still hot.

• The size and shape of jars are often dictated by the type of preserve you are making. Large jars with wide necks are needed for packing whole fruits, whereas smaller ones, 250–500 ml, are more useful for jellies, chutneys, or conserves.

jam tips

• Use ripe or slightly underripe fruit, which contain more pectin and so help the jam to thicken and set.

• Leave any stones in the fruit – when they float to surface, they can be skimmed off the top easily.

• Use a stainless steel or copper preserving pan.

• Seal the jars with a wax disc, pressed down over the jam to remove any air pockets. Top with sterilized lids.

• Store jam in cool, dark place for up to a year. After opening, keep refrigerated or in a cool place out of direct sunlight.

chutney tips

• Use a stainless steel preserving pan – not copper, which will react with the vinegar in some chutneys.

• Seal jars of chutney with a wax disc, smoothed down to remove any air pockets, then a non-metal lid, as the vinegar will corrode metal.

• Store in a cool, dark place for at least a month before eating, to allow flavours to develop and mellow. Unopened jars keep for up to a year, and opened for about a month in the refrigerator or a cool place out of direct sunlight.

strawberry jam

If the strawberries need cleaning, wipe with damp kitchen paper rather than washing them, as the water from washing will affect the jam's consistency.

2 kg strawberries, hulled

freshly squeezed juice of 2 lemons

1.5 kg sugar

*8 preserving jars, 500 ml each,
sterilized (see previous page)*

8 wax discs

makes 8 jars

Put the strawberries and lemon juice into a preserving pan or very large saucepan and heat gently, stirring constantly, until they begin to soften. Add the sugar and heat, stirring, until it has dissolved.

Bring the mixture to the boil then cook, uncovered, at a fast simmer until the setting point is reached, about 8 minutes, testing off the heat for the setting point after 5 minutes.

Remove from the heat and let cool. (If you bottle jam when still hot, the fruit will sink to the bottom.) Skim off any surface foam with a slotted spoon, then stir to redistribute the fruit.

Using a ladle, transfer the jam to sterilized jars and seal with a wax disc, then a lid. Remember to label and date the jars.

To test for setting point: Put 1 teaspoon of jam onto a cold plate and chill for a few minutes. Push your finger gently through it – if the surface wrinkles, the setting point has been reached. If not, return the pan to the heat and boil again, testing again off the heat after a few minutes.

green tomato chutney

Experiment with ingredients for chutney, adjusting the spices and fruits to suit your taste, or adding extras, such as coriander seeds or cloves.

1.5 kg green tomatoes, halved and sliced

500 g tart apples, peeled, cored, quartered and sliced

1 large onion, chopped

1 teaspoon salt

300 ml malt vinegar

175 g soft brown sugar

375 g dates, chopped

250 g sultanas

250 g seedless raisins

2 teaspoons ground ginger

2 teaspoons freshly grated nutmeg

3 teaspoons ground cinnamon

6 preserving jars, 500 ml each, sterilized (see previous page)

6 wax discs

makes 6 jars

Put the tomatoes, apples and onion into a large bowl. Add the salt, mix well, cover and leave overnight.

Put the vinegar and sugar into a preserving pan or very large saucepan and heat gently until the sugar has dissolved. Add the dates, sultanas and raisins, then the prepared tomatoes, apples and onion and heat until boiling. Cover and simmer, stirring frequently, for 2 hours.

Add the ginger, nutmeg and cinnamon and simmer, uncovered, until it is the consistency of thick jam, or until it drops rather than flows from a spoon, 30–60 minutes. Transfer to warm, sterilized jars, let cool and seal with waxed discs, then lids. Remember to label and date the jars.

recipe

ingredients

method

source

recipe

ingredients

method

source

recipe

ingredients

method

source

recipe

ingredients

method

source

christmas turkey

When buying your turkey, allow 500 g per person for a bird that weighs up to 5 kg, or 375 g per person for a larger bird (these weights allow for some leftovers).

1 turkey (see recipe introduction)
150–200 g butter, softened
traditional stuffing (see next page)

a large roasting tin
a small metal skewer

serves 8 or more

Preheat the oven to 180°C (350°F) Gas 4 for a turkey weighing under 6 kg, or 170°C (325°F) Gas 3 for a turkey weighing over 6 kg.

If stuffing the turkey, put breast side up on a board and gently loosen the skin at the neck end. Pack the stuffing into the neck cavity, leaving enough room for it to expand as it cooks, and bring the flap of skin back over the stuffing. Secure with a small metal skewer. Alternatively, put the stuffing into an oven dish, cover with foil and bake in the oven for 30–40 minutes.

Transfer to a large roasting tin and smear the turkey all over with butter. Cover loosely with a double sheet of foil and roast in the preheated oven according to the approximate times given below.

Remove the foil, increase the temperature to 200°C (400°F) Gas 6 and cook for a further 30 minutes to brown and crisp the skin. To test for doneness, push a skewer into the thickest part of a thigh. The juices should run clear and golden. If the juices are at all pink, cook a little longer. If you have a meat thermometer, the internal temperature of the bird should read at least 82°C (180°F).

Remove from the oven and transfer to a warm serving dish. Cover loosely with foil again and let stand for 20–30 minutes to rest before carving.

Note: If using a frozen turkey, it must be thawed thoroughly before cooking. Defrost in the refrigerator according to the times below. (Defrosting poultry at room temperature should be avoided. It can encourage the growth of harmful micro-organisms.)

Approximate defrosting times		Approximate cooking times	
3–5 kg	24 hours	3–5 kg	2½–3½ hours
5–6 kg	24–36 hours	5–6 kg	3½–4¼ hours
7–9 kg	at least 36 hours	7–9 kg	5–6 hours
over 9 kg	at least 48 hours	over 9 kg	at least 6 hours

traditional stuffing

Turkeys cook more quickly and safely without stuffing in the cavity.
Stuff the neck end only and cook the extra stuffing in a baking dish.

2 tablespoons breadcrumbs

8 spring onions, thinly sliced

2 teaspoons chopped fresh rosemary
or 1 teaspoon dried

2 eggs, beaten

1 kg pork sausagemeat

salt and freshly ground black pepper

a short metal skewer

serves 8–10

Put the breadcrumbs in a large bowl and pour over
100 ml boiling water. Set aside and let cool.

Add the spring onions, rosemary, egg and plenty of salt
and pepper and stir to mix.

Add the sausagemeat to the mixture and, using a fork, mix
well. Using your hands, pack the stuffing into the cavity at
the neck end of the bird, allowing room for it to expand as
it cooks. If you have any leftover stuffing, put it in an oven
dish, spread it evenly over the base, then cover with foil
and bake with the turkey for 30–40 minutes.

Pull the flap of skin back over the stuffing and secure with
a short metal skewer.

oven-roasted vegetables

Put into the oven at the same time as the turkey for the last
20 minutes of roasting, then cook for a further 20 minutes while the
turkey rests and you make the gravy.

500 g parsnips, cut into strips

500 g carrots, quartered lengthways

2 red onions, cut into 6 wedges each

1 head of garlic, broken into cloves

3 tablespoons olive or sunflower oil

1 teaspoon sea salt

serves 8–10

Put the parsnips and carrots into a large roasting tin.
Add the red onion wedges, garlic, oil and salt and shake
well to coat. Roast in a preheated oven at 200°C (400°F)
Gas 6 for 40 minutes, turning occasionally until tender
and golden.

Silvana Franco

creamy bread sauce

A classic, delicious accompaniment for turkey. You can make this ahead of time and reheat it but, to stop a skin forming, put clingfilm on the surface of the sauce in the pan. Remove it before reheating.

2 onions, cut into quarters

12 black peppercorns

12 whole cloves

2 bay leaves

500 ml milk

150 g fresh white breadcrumbs

75 g butter

2 tablespoons double cream

salt and freshly ground black pepper

serves 8–10

Put the onion, peppercorns, cloves, bay leaves and milk in a saucepan. Put over a low heat and gently bring to the boil. Remove from the heat and set aside to infuse for approximately 1 hour.

Put the breadcrumbs into a large bowl and strain the infused milk through a sieve into the breadcrumbs. Return the mixture to a clean saucepan. Add the butter and cream and stir over a medium-low heat until thickened. Add salt and pepper to taste.

gravy

Transfer the turkey to a serving dish and let it rest. Use the juices in the roasting tin to make the gravy.

2 tablespoons plain flour

about 300 ml chicken stock

a dash of sherry or Marsala

salt and freshly ground black pepper

serves 8–10

Tip off the fat from the turkey juices in the roasting tin. Remove from the heat and stir in the flour with a balloon whisk.

Put over a low heat and add the stock gradually, stirring constantly, until smooth. Add the sherry or Marsala and salt and pepper to taste and stir for a further 2 minutes.

Pour into a warmed jug and serve with the turkey.

recipe

ingredients

method

source

recipe

ingredients

method

source

party planning countdown

Get organized! Follow the guidelines on this timetable for a smooth, calm, run-up to your party. With nothing to panic about, you can relax and enjoy the preparations and sense of anticipation.

One week ahead

• Order drinks and ice, plus glasses and ice buckets if necessary.

• Assemble all your serving trays and buy or make others if required.

• Arrange candles and music.

• Make sure you have the kitchen equipment required for the menu you've chosen.

• Prepare dishes to be frozen and cooked from frozen or thawed and reheated.

Two to three days ahead

• Prepare those items that can be prepared then kept in an airtight container until just before serving.

• Make ice creams, buy ready-made pastry.

• Write final shopping lists, ordering from specialist shops where necessary.

One day ahead

• Buy all the food, except the most perishable, such as oysters and prawns.

• Prepare meats, sauces and marinades.

• Cook recipes that can be chilled overnight.

• Prepare basic mixtures for macerated drinks such as punch.

• Arrange the room and prepare the bar area, set out glasses, cocktail sticks, napkins, any cocktail equipment and (many) corkscrews and other equipment.

• Check drinks are cold. (Chilling large quantities of drinks at the last minute is asking for trouble!)

• Check straws, linen and napkins.

Morning of party

• Buy foods such as salad leaves, herbs, creams, etc.

• Make remaining dressings and salsas and any herbs or garnishes (float herb sprigs in a bowl of iced water and cover with clingfilm).

• Cut up any vegetables needed for recipes and cover with clingfilm.

• Assemble dishes that are able to stand.

Afternoon of party

• Assemble and cook everything that requires no last-minute preparation and cooking.

Two hours ahead

• Begin cooking and assembling food, and assemble dishes needing last-minute cooking.

Thirty minutes ahead

• Preheat the oven.

• Party should be ready to go and first dishes ready to serve. Uncork wines. Prepare the materials for cocktails. Sit down!

When the first guest arrives

• Pull the champagne corks and take the coats. Serve cocktails and champagne.

cocktail blini

Blini are the one Russian dish that has migrated around the world to smart restaurants and parties everywhere. You can buy cocktail blini in many supermarkets and delicatessens, but usually they're not made authentically with buckwheat flour. Be different!

140 g buckwheat flour
or half-and-half with plain flour

1 sachet (7 g) easy-blend dried yeast

1 teaspoon salt

1 egg, separated

1 teaspoon sugar

170 ml lukewarm milk

1 tablespoon butter, for frying

to serve

crème fraîche or sour cream

herbs, such as snipped chives
and dill sprigs

small pots of caviar and/or salmon roe

about 4 pieces smoked salmon,
finely sliced

makes 24

Mix the flour, yeast and salt in a bowl and make a well in the centre. Whisk the egg yolk with the sugar and 170 ml warm water and add to the well. Mix well, then cover with a damp cloth and let rise at room temperature until doubled in size, about 2 hours.

Beat in the milk to make a thick, creamy batter. Cover again and leave for 1 hour until small bubbles appear on the surface. Beat the egg white to soft peak stage, then fold it into the batter.

Heat a heavy-based frying pan or crêpe pan, and brush with butter. Drop in about 1 teaspoon of batter to make a pancake about 2.5 cm in diameter. Cook until the surface bubbles, about 2–3 minutes, then flip the blin over with a palette knife and cook the second side for about 2 minutes.

Put on a plate in the oven to keep warm while you cook the remaining blini. (Don't put them on top of each other.) Serve warm.

To serve, top with a spoonful of crème fraîche, some chives or dill and a small pile of caviar or roe or a curl of smoked salmon.

• Store in an airtight container for up to 3 days.

• Reheat for 5 minutes in a preheated oven at 200°C (400°F) Gas 6.

Elsa Petersen-Schepelern

parties

recipe

ingredients

method

source

recipe

ingredients

method

source

margarita

The Margarita is the cocktail most closely associated with tequila. This is the classic recipe, but when you are making it at home there is no right or wrong way – just your way!

50 ml gold tequila

25 ml triple sec (or Cointreau)

juice of ½ lime

a cocktail shaker

Shake all the ingredients with cracked ice. Strain into a chilled cocktail glass rimmed with salt.

sea breeze

The cranberry juice lends a light, fruity and slightly bitter quality to this classic vodka-based cocktail.

50 ml vodka

cranberry juice

fresh grapefruit juice

a shot measure

Pour a large shot of vodka into a highball glass filled with ice. Three quarters fill the glass with cranberry juice and top with fresh grapefruit juice. Garnish with a lime quarter and serve with a straw.

bloody mary

A great hangover cure, but if you can't face alcohol, skip the vodka and make it a Virgin Mary instead.

50 ml vodka

200 ml tomato juice

2 grinds of black pepper

2 dashes of Worcestershire sauce

2 dashes of Tabasco sauce

2 dashes of fresh lemon juice

1 barspoon horseradish sauce

1 celery stick

a cocktail shaker

Shake all the ingredients over ice and strain into a highball glass filled with ice. (These measurements are dependent on personal likes or dislikes for spices.)

champagne cocktail

A simple and delicious cocktail – as popular now as when it was sipped by stars of the silver screen in the 1940s.

25 ml brandy

1 white sugar cube

2 dashes of Angostura bitters

dry champagne

Moisten the sugar cube with Angostura bitters and put in a champagne flute. Add the brandy, then gently pour in the champagne and serve.

Ben Reed

recipe

ingredients

method

source

recipe

ingredients

method

source

recipe

ingredients

method

source

recipe

ingredients

method

source

dinner party notes

Avoid cooking the same dish twice for the same people – keep a
record of everything you cook for guests. Use the comments space to
make notes on timings, preparation and quantities. For future use,
photocopy this page before you start, so you don't run out of room.

date

guests

menu

comments

date

guests

menu

comments

dinner party notes

date

guests

menu

comments

---

date

guests

menu

comments

---

date

guests

menu

comments

dinner party notes

date

guests

menu

comments

date

guests

menu

comments

date

guests

menu

comments

conversion chart

Stick to one system when measuring. Measure
liquids in a jug set on a flat surface. When using
cups, spoon the ingredient into the measuring cup
and level off with a knife. Weights and measures
have been rounded up or down slightly to make
measuring easier.

Volume equivalents:

American	Metric	Imperial
1 teaspoon	5 ml	
1 tablespoon	15 ml	
¼ cup	60 ml	2 fl.oz.
⅓ cup	75 ml	2½ fl.oz.
½ cup	125 ml	4 fl.oz.
⅔ cup	150 ml	5 fl.oz. (¼ pint)
¾ cup	175 ml	6 fl.oz.
1 cup	250 ml	8 fl.oz.
1¼ cups	300 ml	10 fl.oz.
1⅓ cups	325 ml	11 fl.oz.
1½ cups	350 ml	12 fl.oz.
1⅔ cups	375 ml	13 fl.oz.
1¾ cups	400 ml	14 fl.oz.
2 cups	500 ml	16 fl.oz.

Weight equivalents: Measurements:

Imperial	Metric	Inches	Cm
1 oz.	25 g	¼ inch	5 mm
2 oz.	50 g	½ inch	1 cm
3 oz.	75 g	¾ inch	1.5 cm
4 oz.	125 g	1 inch	2.5 cm
5 oz.	150 g	2 inches	5 cm
6 oz.	175 g	3 inches	7 cm
7 oz.	200 g	4 inches	10 cm
8 oz. (½ lb.)	250 g	5 inches	12 cm
9 oz.	275 g	6 inches	15 cm
10 oz.	300 g	7 inches	18 cm
11 oz.	325 g	8 inches	20 cm
12 oz.	375 g	9 inches	23 cm
13 oz.	400 g	10 inches	25 cm
14 oz.	425 g	11 inches	28 cm
15 oz.	475 g	12 inches	30 cm
16 oz. (1 lb.)	500 g		
2 1b.	1 kg		

Oven temperatures:

110°C	(225°F)	Gas ¼
120°C	(250°F)	Gas ½
140°C	(275°F)	Gas 1
150°C	(300°F)	Gas 2
160°C	(325°F)	Gas 3
180°C	(350°F)	Gas 4
190°C	(375°F)	Gas 5
200°C	(400°F)	Gas 6
220°C	(425°F)	Gas 7
230°C	(450°F)	Gas 8
240°C	(475°F)	Gas 9

credits

Senior Designer Steve Painter

Commissioning Editor
Elsa Petersen-Schepelern

Editor Sally Somers

Production Deborah Wehner

Art Director Gabriella Le Grazie

Publishing Director Alison Starling

First published in Great Britain in 2001
by Ryland Peters & Small
20–21 Jockey's Fields
London WC1R 4BW
www.rylandpeters.com

10 9 8

Photographs by: Martin Brigdale, Peter Cassidy,
Jeremy Hopley, William Lingwood, Jason Lowe, James
Merrell, Peter Myers, Debi Treloar, Patrice de Villiers,
Philip Webb, Simon Wheeler and Alan Williams.

ISBN-10: 1 84172 214 6
ISBN-13: 978 1 84172 214 6

A CIP record for this book is available from
the British Library.

Printed and bound in China

Notes

All spoon measurements are level unless
otherwise noted.

Ovens should be preheated to the specified
temperature. Recipes in this book were tested
with a fan-assisted oven. If using a regular oven,
increase the cooking times according to the
manufacturer's instructions.

Specialist Asian ingredients are available in large
supermarkets, Thai and Chinese shops, as well
as Asian stores.

Soft cheeses and uncooked or partly cooked eggs
should not be served to the very old or frail, the very
young or to pregnant women.

Classic Vinaigrette and Rare Beef Salad with Parsley
and Wasabi Mayonnaise from **Salads** by *Elsa
Petersen-Schepelern*, photography by *Peter Cassidy*

Pumpkin Soup with Pumpkin Crisps from
Pumpkin, Butternut and Squash by *Elsa Petersen-
Schepelern*, photography by *Debi Treloar*

Roasted Chicken from **Chicken: from Maryland
to Kiev** by *Clare Ferguson*, photography by
Peter Cassidy

Char-Grilled Pork and Aubergine, Marinades and Rubs
and Grill Pan Tips from **Grill Pan Cooking** by *Elsa
Petersen-Schepelern*, photography by *Peter Cassidy*

Barbecued Salmon Steaks with Basil and Parmesan
Butter from **Salmon** by *Maxine Clark*, photography by
William Lingwood

Classic Tomato Sauce, Pesto and Chocolate Chunk
Nut Cookies from **New Vegetarian** by *Celia Brooks
Brown*, photography by *Philip Webb*

Risotto with Four Cheeses from **Risotto** by *Ursula
Ferrigno*, photography by *Jason Lowe*

Chilled Soba Noodle Salad from **Big Bowl** by *Elsa
Petersen-Schepelern*, photography by *Jeremy Hopley*

Spanish Roasted Vegetables from **Extra Virgin:
Cooking with Olive Oil** by *Clare Ferguson*,
photography by *Peter Cassidy*

Gooey Brownies and Chocolate Tips
from **Heavenly Chocolate** by *Linda Collister*,
photography by *Debi Treloar*

Basic Sweet Tart, Lemon Filling and Apple and Berry
Deep Dish Pie from **Sweet Pies and Tarts** by *Linda
Collister*, photography by *Patrice de Villiers*

Blackberry and Raspberry Sorbet from **Gelati,
Sorbets and Ice Creams** by *Elsa Petersen-
Schepelern*, photography by *James Merrell*

Party Planning Countdown and Cocktail Blini from
Finger Food by *Elsa Petersen-Schepelern*,
photography by *William Lingwood*

Margarita, Bloody Mary, Sea Breeze and Champagne
Cocktail from **Cool Cocktails** by *Ben Reed*,
photography by *William Lingwood*

Rice Types and Cooking Times from **Rice: from
Risotto to Sushi** by *Clare Ferguson*, photography
by *Jeremy Hopley*

Noodle Types and Cooking Times from **Noodles and
Pasta** by *Joy Davies*, photography by *Simon Wheeler*

All published by Ryland Peters & Small